PRINTING PRACTICE
HANDWRITING
WORKBOOK FOR BOYS

JULIE HARPER

Printing Practice Handwriting Workbook for Boys

Cover Design by Melissa Stevens
www.theillustratedauthor.net
Write. Create. Illustrate.

Children's Books > Education & Reference > Words & Language

Children's Books > Education & Reference > Education > Workbooks

ISBN 10: 150019994X

EAN 13: 978-1500199944

Table of Contents

Introduction

The goal of this workbook is to inspire boys' interest in learning and practicing print handwriting. Boys enjoy reading phrases like, "No girls allowed," and sentences like, "Meet me at the secret clubhouse." Exercises like these help to make learning fun, whether in the classroom or at home.

This *Printing Practice Handwriting Workbook for Boys* focuses on writing phrases and sentences in print. Students who need more practice writing individual letters or single words may benefit from using this workbook in combination with a basic print writing workbook which focuses on practicing letters and short words.

Three sections of this workbook help students develop their print writing skills in four parts:

- ✓ Part 1 focuses on tracing and copying words and short phrases.

- ✓ Part 2 has longer phrases and short sentences to trace and copy.

- ✓ Part 3 consists of longer sentences. There is no tracing in Part 3.

- ✓ Part 4 provides short writing exercises.

May your students or children improve their handwriting skills and enjoy reading and writing these phrases and sentences.

Uppercase Alphabet

A B C D E F

G H I J K L

M N O P Q R

S T U V W X

Y Z

Lowercase Alphabet

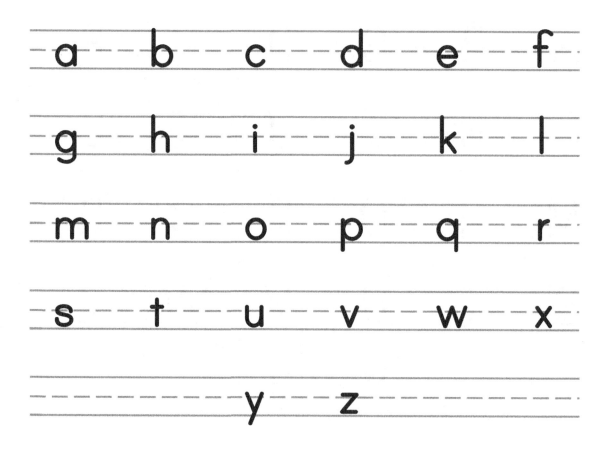

a b c d e f

g h i j k l

m n o p q r

s t u v w x

y z

Part 1 Words and Short Phrases

Part 1 instructions: First trace each word or short phrase and then copy the words onto the blank line below.

Treehouse

treehouse

Climbing

Climbing

Boys only

Boys only

Password

password

Code name

Code name

Members

Members

Private

private

Keep out

Keepout

Secret handshake

Secret hand shake

Hidden entrance

Hidden entrance

Camouflage

Camoufage

Exclusive

Exclusive

Girls not allowed

Girls not allowed

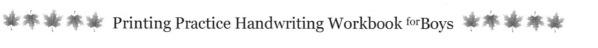

Club meeting

Roll call

Agenda

Leadership

Special assignment

Scavenger hunt

Riddles and clues

Magnifying glass

Treasure hunt

Competition

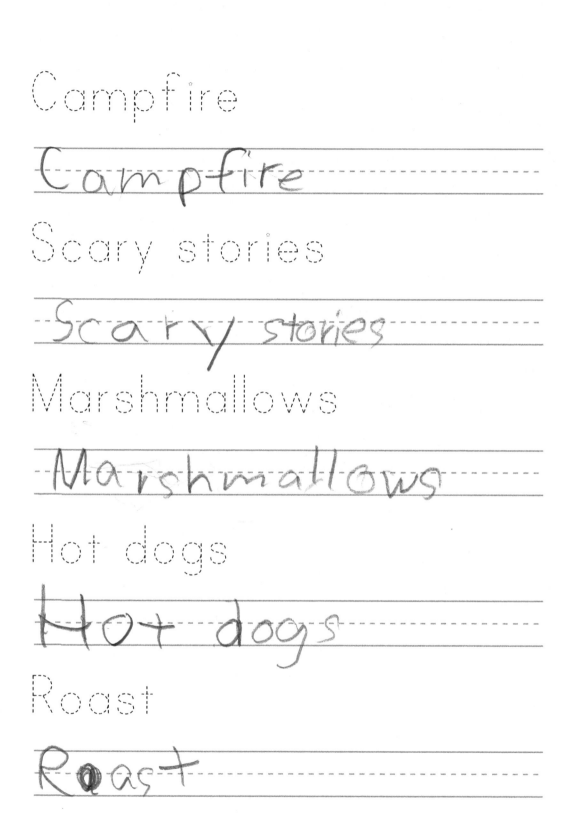

Campfire

Campfire

Scary stories

Scary stories

Marshmallows

Marshmallows

Hot dogs

Hot dogs

Roast

Roast

Boy scouts

Survival

Wilderness

Compass

Earn badges

Find a clearing

Set up camp

Open backpack

Pitch the tent

Unroll sleeping bags

Hiking trails

Nature walks

Back country

Rock climbing

River rafting

Insects and spiders

Insects and spiders

Butterflies

Butterflies

Slimy worms

Slimy worms

Centipedes

Centider

Tarantulas

Tarantulas

President

president

Vice-President

Vice-president

Treasurer

Treasurer

Secretary

Secretary

Special Agent

Special Agent

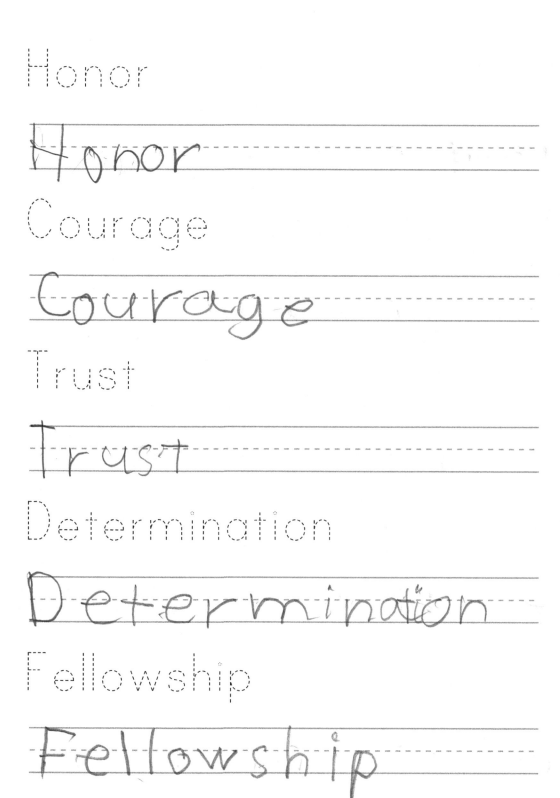

Honor

Honor

Courage

Courage

Trust

Trust

Determination

Determination

Fellowship

Fellowship

Super heroes

Super heroes

Special powers

Special powers

Crime fighters

Crime fighters

Secret identity

Secret identity

Cool costume

Cool costume

Game night

Marbles

Board game

Cards or dice

Checkers or chess

Collections

Baseball cards

Merit badges

Trophy case

Rocks, bugs, leaves

Movie time

Popcorn

Soda pop

DVD player

Quiet, please

Pirate ship

Treasure chest

Crossbones

Talking parrots

Walk the plank

Ahoy, mateys

Blimey

You landlubbers

Swab the deck

Fire in the hole

Favorite pets

Cats or dogs

Hamsters or parrots

Lizards or snakes

Fish tank

Video games

Joystick

Console

Controller

Cartridges

Arcade games

Tokens

Prizes

Racing

High score

Miniature golf

Ramps and tunnels

Windmill obstacle

Putting surface

Colored golf balls

Outdoor sports

Baseball or football

Hockey or basketball

Soccer or frisbee

Tag or hide-n-seek

Extreme sports

Snowboarding

Skate park

Mountain biking

Zip line

Exercise

Gymnastics

Push-ups

Chin-ups

Cartwheels

Stargazing

Full moon

Solar eclipse

Meteor shower

Constellations

Solar system

Milky Way

Asteroid belt

Kuiper belt

Comets

The planets...

Mercury and Venus

Earth and Mars

Jupiter and Saturn

Uranus and Neptune

Scary monsters

Frankenstein

Vampires

Werewolves

Skeletons

Jet airplane

Stunt plane

Bomber

Hang glider

Parachute

Aircraft carrier

Submarine

Sailboat

Cargo ship

Cruise liner

Delivery truck

Eighteen-wheeler

Semi-trailer truck

Cement mixer

Flatbed truck

Four-wheel drive

Off-road

All-terrain

Outdoor

Vehicle

Race cars

Drag racing

Demolition derby

Stock cars

Grand Prix

Emergency vehicles

Police car

Fire engine

Rescue squad

Ambulance

Dragons

Fire-breathing

Cloud-soaring

Serpentine

Strong scales

Origami

Paper airplanes

House of cards

Model volcano

Popsicle stick sculpture

Arts and crafts

Watercolor

Finger painting

Blueprints

Model airplane

Martial Arts

Judo and Kung Fu

Karate

Kickboxing

Black belt

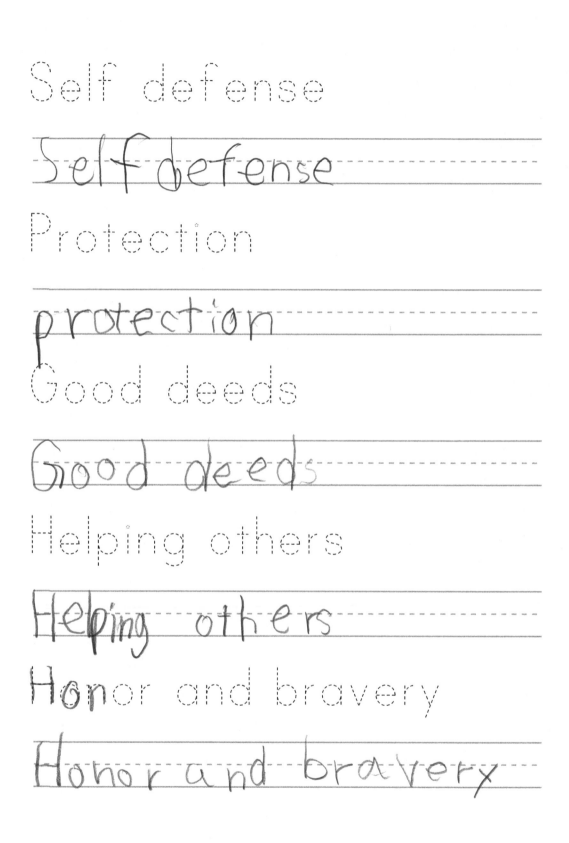

Self defense

Self defense

Protection

protection

Good deeds

Good deeds

Helping others

Helping others

Honor and bravery

Honor and bravery

Summer camp

Summer camp

Activities

Activities

Competition

Competition

Sports

Sports

Teamwork

teamwork

Team player

Leadership

Model behavior

Bond together

Support one another

Part 2 Short Sentences

Part 2 instructions: First trace the words of these phrases and short sentences and then copy the words onto the blank line below.

Climb the rope ladder.

Knock three times.

Enter the clubhouse.

It's a special time.

Play with your friends.

Make up new games.

Enjoy time together.

Discuss your ideas.

My secret clubhouse...

Boys only!

Girls are not allowed.

Private property.

By invitation only...

Explore caves...

Watch out for bats.

It's dark and cool.

Don't slip and fall.

Find a cave spider.

Tag, you're it!

Have a treasure hunt.

Toss a football.

Jump up and down

on a trampoline.

Weekends are for...

Hanging with friends.

Playing video games.

Tossing a Frisbee.

Throwing a football.

Let's see who can...

Run the fastest.

Jump the farthest.

Yell the loudest.

Climb the highest.

Walk your dog.

Teach him a trick.

Give him a bone.

Play tug-of-war.

Good doggie!

Born to play sports...

Play to win.

Learn from losing.

Train hard.

Don't give up!

Be a good sport.

Give it your best shot.

It takes teamwork.

Winning and losing...

It's all about fun!

Whistle a tune.

Beat the drums.

Strum a guitar.

Sing in the shower.

Play the saxophone.

Bait the hook.

Cast your line.

Wait for a bite.

Reel the fish in.

Release the fish!

A day at the arcade...

Ride the bumper cars.

Race the mini cars.

Play video games.

Eat lots of pizza.

Playing in the snow...

Throw snowballs.

Build snowmen.

Make snow angels.

Try to stay warm.

Pizza for breakfast!

Ice-cream for dinner!

Cookies any time!

Dessert, then dinner!

Cereal for lunch!

A day at the races...

Start your engines...

It's super fast!

Zoom, zoom, zoom!

Take a victory lap.

Are you competitive?

Do you play for fun?

It's okay to lose.

Practice and enjoy.

Be prepared.

Fun at the pool.

Dive for coins.

Race across the pool.

Play water tag.

Practice your dive.

Off to a ballgame...

Root for your team.

Eat hotdogs.

Yell and cheer.

Catch a foul ball.

Go skateboarding.

Ride the ramps.

Compete with friends.

Do some tricks.

Wear protective gear.

Swing at the park.

Feed the ducks.

Go down a slide.

Run and play.

Have a picnic.

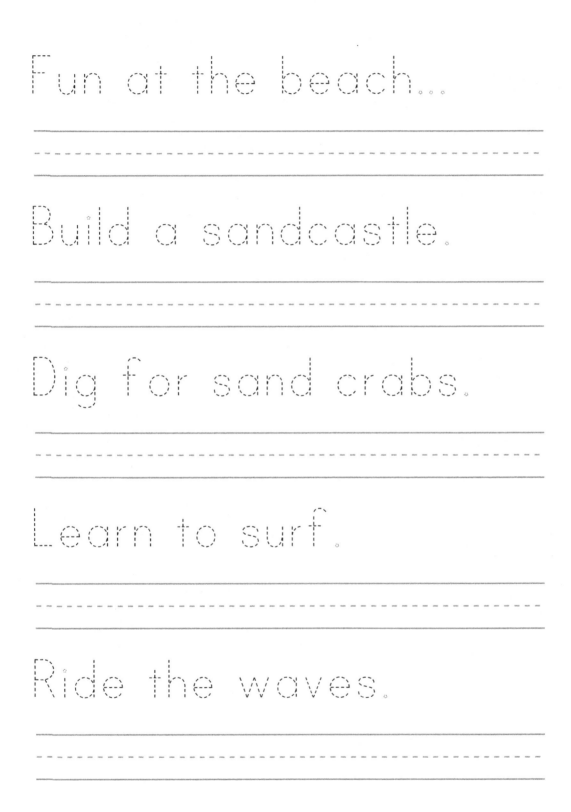

Fun at the beach...

Build a sandcastle.

Dig for sand crabs.

Learn to surf.

Ride the waves.

It's hot outside.

Go to the waterpark.

Ride the slides.

Twist and turn.

Splash your friends.

I can do it!

No excuses.

I believe in myself!

It can be done!

I know I can do it!

Do you like bugs?

Creepy spiders...

Stinging scorpions...

Hairy tarantulas...

Slimy slugs...

Arrrr... It's a pirate.

Sail the blue seas.

I see a pirate ship.

Aargh! Yo-ho-ho!

X marks the spot.

Yodel in the hills...

Whisper a secret.

Yell until it echoes...

Sing in the rain.

Whistle a happy tune.

Summer camp fun...

Sleep under the stars.

Have a wiener roast.

Tell ghost stories.

Have some s'mores.

Hop, skip, and jump.

Jump over hurdles.

Do one-legged jumps.

Jump the highest.

Jump the farthest.

The referee...

Throws a flag.

Blows the whistle.

Calls a penalty.

Supervises the game.

Miniature golf is fun.

Lots of obstacles!

Hit a bank shot.

Make a hole-in-one.

Be the best putter.

Let's go skating...

The rink is open.

Get your rollerblades.

Can you skate on one

foot or backwards?

What's your favorite

pizza topping?

Is it pepperoni,

onions, extra cheese,

sausage, or olives?

Are you hungry for...

a cheeseburger?

a chili dog and fries?

a bag of chips?

or something else?

Part 3 Just Copy

Part 3 instructions: Just copy the words of these sentences onto the blank lines below. There is no tracing in Part 3.

What will we do today?

Play hard from sunrise

to sunset. Start now!

Adventurous boys

love to climb trees,

explore the outdoors,

discover new things,

and have fun.

Spy games are fun!

You can sneak

around, catch enemy

spies, and save

your neighborhood.

My friends and I

write secret notes

with invisible ink so

we are the only ones

who can read them.

Build a tree house.

What would be your

ideal tree fort?

Design it yourself.

Keep it locked!

A tent made out of

blankets is my special

hideout. It's my private

place when I need

some alone time.

We love spending

time outdoors rock

climbing, hiking, and

running barefoot

through the grass.

Gone fishing!

I'm ready to cast my

line, and reel in one

fish after another!

Let's catch the limit!

It's fun to have

water balloon fights

with my friends on

hot summer days.

Don't stay dry!

It's a boys versus

girls tug-of-war

contest. The score is

1 to 1. Get ready for

the tiebreaker.

It would be so cool

to have super powers.

Imagine being able to

fly or being super

strong. Save the world!

What would you do if

you discovered that

you had magic powers?

What kind of spells

would you like to cast?

It would be fun to

discover a dragon egg,

watch it hatch, and

keep it for a pet.

I want to fly one.

But what if the dragon

could breathe fire?

That might be a

problem. One sneeze

could burn the house!

Can you jump on

a pogo stick with a

parrot on your

shoulder while playing

a harmonica?

Try rubbing your tummy

in a circle while patting

your head. While doing

that, jump up and down

and spin around, too!

Can you play a

musical instrument?

Can you carry a tune?

It's time to join a

band or choir.

Friday night is my

favorite time to

play a board game,

listen to music, or

read a book.

Fly a kite on a windy

afternoon. How high

can it fly? The wind

will carry it as it

reaches for the sky.

Surf's up! Grab your

surfboard and catch

some waves. Ride the

wave out. But don't go

near the rocks.

Do you know who could

eat five hundred

pounds of meat in

one bite? The answer

is Tyrannosaurus Rex.

That would be like

shoving a thousand

cheeseburgers into

your mouth all in a

singe bite. Wow!

Do you know how to

find the North Star,

Polaris, in the night

sky? How about the

Big and Little Dippers?

Have you ever seen

a comet or a meteor

shower? What about

a solar or a lunar

eclipse?

Part 4 Writing Exercises

Part 4 instructions: Write answers to these questions in the space provided.

Exercise 1. Where is your favorite hideout?

Exercise 2. Describe your favorite hideout.

Exercise 3. List the names of your friends.

Exercise 4. List things you like to do with your friends.

Exercise 5. Describe something fun that you did with your friends.

Exercise 6. Which kinds of bugs can you think of?

Exercise 7. What is something cool you could do if you were a bug?

Exercise 8. What would be dangerous about being a bug?

Exercise 9. Which kinds of trucks can you think of?

Exercise 10. If you could drive your favorite truck, where would you go?

Exercise 11. What paint color, wheels, and features would it have?

Exercise 12. List your favorite sports.

Exercise 13. Describe your favorite memory with sports.

Exercise 14. How does your favorite sport help you as a person?

Exercise 15. Where would you like to go on vacation?

Exercise 16. What would you like to do there?

Exercise 17. Would you like to live there? Why or why not?

Exercise 18. Try to name all the planets.

Exercise 19. Which planet would you like to visit? Why?

Exercise 20. Do you believe UFO's exist? Why or why not?

Exercise 21. What does the word "monster" mean to you?

Exercise 22. Invent a new kind of monster. Name it and describe it.

Exercise 23. What would it be like to be that monster?

Exercise 24. List some types of dinosaurs that you know of.

Exercise 25. Describe your favorite dinosaur.

Exercise 26. What would it be like to live with dinosaurs?

Exercise 27. List some things that you're good at.

Exercise 28. Pick one. How do you know you're good at it?

Exercise 29. Describe something that you wish you could do better.

Exercise 30. List your favorite zoo animals.

Exercise 31. Describe your favorite zoo animal.

Exercise 32. What would it be like to live in a zoo?

Exercise 33. Which games can you think of?

Exercise 34. Describe your favorite game.

Exercise 35. What makes this game so fun?

Exercise 36. List some ridiculous pizza toppings (like ice-cream).

Exercise 37. Write something really ridiculous.

Exercise 38. Describe something ridiculous that you've seen before.

Exercise 39. Describe what you want to be when you grow up.

Exercise 40. Describe what that would be like.

Exercise 41. What do you need to do to make that happen?

Exercise 42. List creatures that live in the ocean.

Exercise 43. Describe your favorite ocean animal.

Exercise 44. What would it be like to live in the ocean?

Exercise 45. What is your favorite video game?

Exercise 46. Describe your favorite video game.

Exercise 47. What is the best thing you've done in that game?

Exercise 48. Which tools can you think of?

Exercise 49. Describe something you could build with those tools.

Exercise 50. What would be the hardest parts about building it?

Exercise 51. List subjects that you study in school.

Exercise 52. Describe your favorite subject.

Exercise 53. Describe your favorite teacher.

Exercise 54. What do you like most about your father?

Exercise 55. Describe something fun you did with your father.

Exercise 56. Describe something special that you did for your father.

Exercise 57. What do you like most about your mother?

Exercise 58. Describe something fun you did with your mother.

Exercise 59. Describe something special that you did for your mother.

Exercise 60. List your favorite snacks.

Exercise 61. Describe what it's like to eat your favorite snack.

Exercise 62. Describe your least favorite food.

Exercise 63. List things you could do at an amusement park.

Exercise 64. Describe your favorite amusement park.

Exercise 65. Describe your favorite movie.

Cursive Handwriting Practice for Boys

Cursive Handwriting Practice for Teens

Julie Harper's Workbooks

www.wackysentences.com

Printing Practice:

- ✓ Printing Practice Handwriting Workbook for Girls.
- ✓ Printing Practice Handwriting Workbook for Boys.
- ✓ Tongue Twisters Printing Practice Writing Workbook.
- ✓ Print Uppercase and Lowercase Letters, Words, and Silly Phrases: Kindergarten and First Grade Writing Practice Workbook (Reproducible).
- ✓ Print Wacky Sentences: First and Second Grade Writing Practice Workbook (Reproducible).

Cursive Handwriting:

- ✓ Letters, Words, and Silly Phrases Handwriting Workbook (Reproducible): Practice Writing in Cursive (Second and Third Grade).
- ✓ Wacky Sentences Handwriting Workbook (Reproducible): Practice Writing in Cursive (Third and Fourth Grade).
- ✓ Cursive Handwriting Workbook for Girls.
- ✓ Cursive Handwriting Practice Workbook for Teens.
- ✓ Spooky Cursive Handwriting Practice Workbook.
- ✓ Cursive Handwriting Practice Workbook for Boys.

Reading & Writing:

- ✓ Reading Comprehension for Girls.
- ✓ Read Wacky Sentences Basic Reading Comprehension Workbook.
- ✓ Wacky Creative Writing Assignments Workbook.

Made in the USA
Middletown, DE
13 August 2020